Presented to:

Never Forget The Difference You've Made

Made in United States
Troutdale, OR
11/27/2023

15030166R00066